D0905198

Folk Songs for Solo Singers

11 Folk Songs Arranged for Solo Voice and Piano...
For Recitals, Concerts and Contests

COMPILED AND EDITED BY JAY ALTHOUSE

Contents

Cover art: Ralph Wheelock's Farm
by Francis Alexander (American, 1800–1880)
oil on canvas, c. 1822
Gift of Edgar William and Bernice Chrysler Garbisch
© 1993 National Gallery of Art, Washington

Alfred

Art Direction: Ted Engelbart
Cover Design: Susan H. Hartman

Many of the vocal solos in *Folk Songs for Solo Singers* are also available in choral editions from Alfred Publishing Co., Inc.

Amazing Grace, arranged by Jay Althouse
    SATB 4792
    3-part mixed 4793

Angels through the Night, arranged by Philip Kern
    SATB 7775
    SSA 7774

'Cross the Wide Missouri, arranged by Don Besig, with additional words by Nancy Price
    SATB 4752
    3-part mixed 4753
    SSA 4754
    2-part 4755

Danny Boy, arranged by Julie Knowles
    SATB 7903
    3-part mixed 7904
    SSA 7684
    2-part 7905

Farewell, Lad (Adéu Donzellet), arranged by Jackie O'Neill
    SSA 5766

Homeward Bound, by Marta Keen, arranged by Jay Althouse
    SATB 7845
    SSA 7846

Liza Jane, arranged by Jay Althouse
    SATB 7376

She's Like the Swallow, arranged by Carl Strommen
    SATB 7878
    SSA 7879

To the Sky, arranged by Carl Strommen
    SATB 7762
    SSA 7763

Order these Alfred choral editions from your favorite music dealer.

AMAZING GRACE

3

Words by
JOHN NEWTON

Early American Melody
Arranged by JAY ALTHOUSE

13
once _____ was ___ lost but now _____ am found was

17
poco rit.   *a tempo*
blind, but ___ now I see. _____

21   *mf*   **23**
Through man - y ___ dan - gers

25
toils and snares, I have al - read - y

come._____ 'Tis grace _____ hath

brought me safe _____ thus _____ far, and

grace will ___ lead me home.

GREENSLEEVES

English Traditional Song
Arranged by PHILIP KERN

Note: Optional bell part on page 12.

GREENSLEEVES

BELLS

English Traditional Song
Arranged by PHILIP KERN

'LIZA JANE

Folksong

Adapted and Arranged by JAY ALTHOUSE

Copyright © MCMXCIII by Alfred Publishing Co., Inc.

on my door, ___ oh, E - li - za Jane.

I got a house in Bal - ti - more, _ oh, 'Li - za Jane;

street - car ___ runs right by my door, __ oh, E - li - za

FAREWELL, LAD

(Adéu Donzellet)

Catalan Folk Song
Arrangement and English lyrics
by JACKIE O'NEILL

* Catalan pronunciation guide on p. 22.

25
hand - some, be - comes a sol - dier in days of war.
tat i tan e - le - gant que s'en va a sol - dat.

28
mf 29
Re - turn when the fight - ing's o'er when your cap - tain
Jo di - ré al ca - pi - tà que em dei - xi tor -
mf

31
cresc. *f*
brave needs you there no more._____ Re -
nar, a la me - va ter - ra;_____ jo
cresc.

34
turn when the fight - ing's o'er; I'll be wait - ing
di - ré al ca - pi - tà que em dei - xi tor -
f

here, here in Vi - las - sar. * Re -
nar *cap* *a* *Vi* - *las* - *sar.* *Jo*

turn when the fight - ing's o'er; I'll be wait - ing
di - *ré* *al* *ca* - *pi* - *tà,* *que* *em* *dei* - *xi* *tor* -

here, here in Vi - las - sar.
nar *cap* *a* *Vi* - *las* - *sar.*

* Vilassar - a seacoast town in Catalonia, north of Barcelona.

ABOUT THE COMPOSITION

This ancient folk song is from the northeastern area of Spain known as Catalonia, bordering on France and the Mediterranean. The original lyrics are in Catalan, a romance language evolving from the ancient southern French language, "Langue d'oc."

PRONUNCIATION GUIDE
Adéu Donzellet

1. Adéu,   donzellet,   adéu,
   (Ah-dayoo, doon-zeh-yet, ah-dayoo,)
   que si tu te'n vas quedaré   soleta;
   (keh see too tahn vahs keh-dah-R̃eh soo-leh-tah;)
   adéu,   donzellet,   adéu,
   (ah-dayoo, doon-zeh-yet, ah-dayoo,)
   que si tu te'n vas ja   no tornaràs.
   (keh see too tahn vahs zhah* noh touR̃-nah-R̃ahs.)

2. Aquell noi tan ben plantat   i tan elegant
   (Ah-kay noy tahn behn plahn-taht ee tahn eh-leh-gahn)
   que se'n va a la guerra?
   (keh sehn vah͡ah lah geh-R̃ah?)
   Aquell noi tan ben plantat   i tan elegant
   (Ah-kay noy tahn behn plahn-taht ee tahn eh-leh-gahn)
   que se'n va a soldat.
   (keh sehn vah͡ah sool-daht.)

3. Jo   diré   al capità   que em deixi   tornar
   (Zhoh* dee-R̃ay ahl kah-pee-tah keh͡ehm day-shee touR̃-nah)
   a la meva   terra;
   (ah lah meh-vah teh-R̃ah;)
   jo   diré   al capità,   que em deixi   tornar
   (zhoh* dee-R̃ay ahl kah-pee-tah, keh͡ehm day-shee touR̃-nah)
   cap a Vilassar.
   (kahp ah Vee-lah-sah.)

* — "zh" equals the French pronunciation of "J" as in "Je" or "Jacques."
NOTE: Rolled R's are indicated by " ~ " over the letter "R."

DANNY BOY

Old Irish Air
Arranged by JULIE KNOWLES

Words by FRED E. WEATHERLY

here in sun-shine or in shad - ow, _____ Oh, Dan - ny

Boy, oh Dan - ny Boy, I love you so!

But when ye

come, and all the flow'rs are dy - ing, _____ and I am

24 dead, as dead I well may be, Ye'll come and

26 find the place where I am ly - ing, and kneel and

28 say an A - ve there for me; And I shall

30 *mf* hear, tho' soft you tread a - bove ___ me, ___ and all my

grave will warm - er, sweet - er be, _____ for you will bend, and tell me that you love ____ me, _____ and I shall sleep in peace un - til you come to me! Oh, Dan - ny Boy, oh Dan - ny Boy, I love you so!

TO THE SKY

Adapted from "Prospect,"
a Southern Folk Song
by CARL STROMMEN

To the sky from the earth in loft - y ___

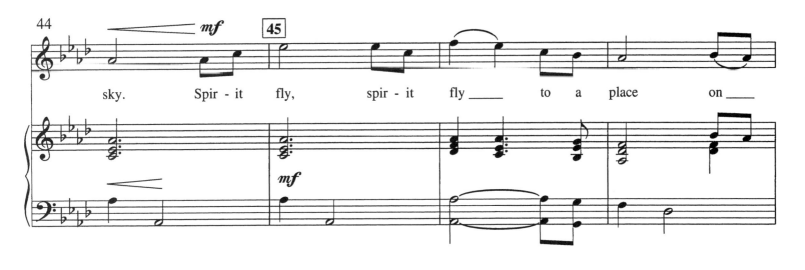

sky. Spir - it fly, spir - it fly ___ to a place on ___

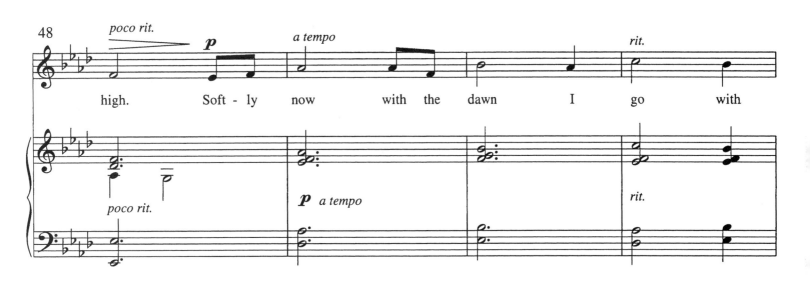

high. Soft - ly now with the dawn I go with

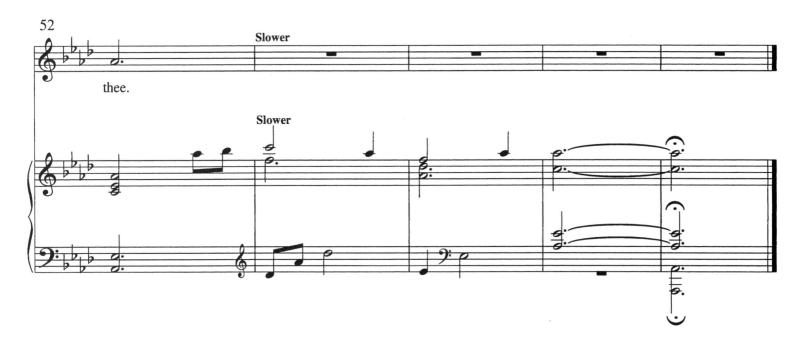

thee.

SCARBOROUGH FAIR

English Folksong
Arranged by JAY ALTHOUSE

Are you goin' to Scar - bor-ough Fair?
Tell her to make me a cam - bric shirt,

Pars - ley, sage, rose - mar - y and thyme.
Pars - ley, sage, rose - mar - y and thyme.

19

Re - mem - ber me to one who lives
With - out a seam or nee - dle

23

there, _____ For once she was a true love of
work, _____ For once she was a true love of

27

1.

mine. _____

f

32

SHE'S LIKE THE SWALLOW

Newfoundland Folk Song
Arranged by CARL STROMMEN

Tenderly (♩ = ca. 84-88)

(pedal carefully throughout)

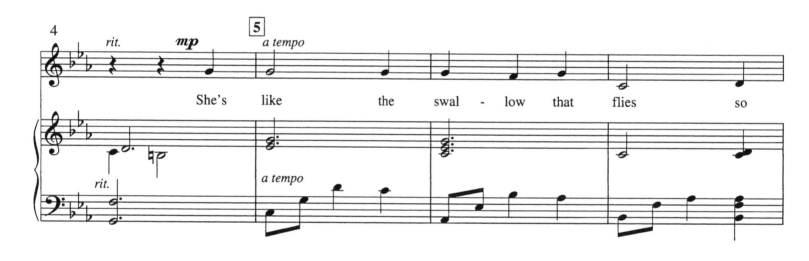

She's like the swal-low that flies so

high. She's like the riv-er that nev-er runs

* lee: sheltered from the wind

ANGELS THROUGH THE NIGHT

(All Through the Night/All Night, All Day)

Traditional
Arranged by PHILIP KERN

Moderately, with feeling (♩ = ca. 92)

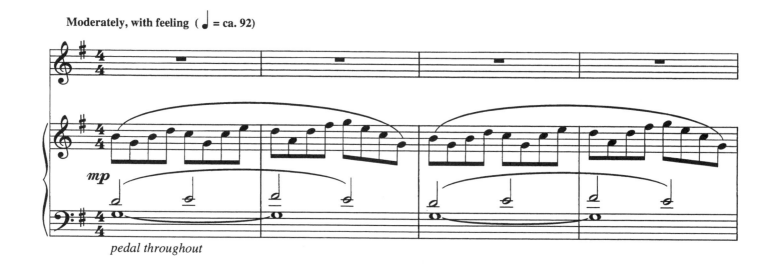

pedal throughout

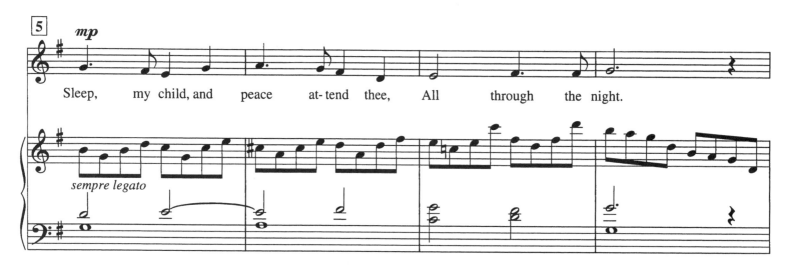

Sleep, my child, and peace at-tend thee, All through the night.

sempre legato

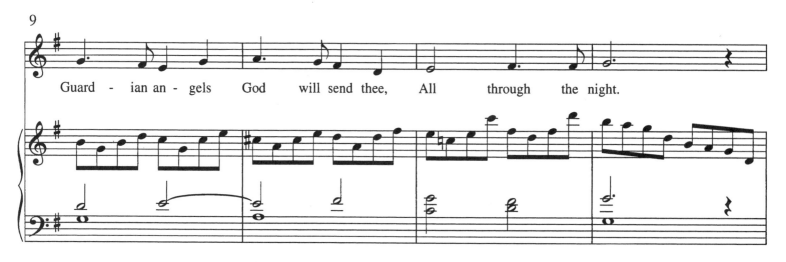

Guard - ian an - gels God will send thee, All through the night.

HOMEWARD BOUND

Arranged by
JAY ALTHOUSE

Words and Music by
MARTA KEEN

Tenderly (♩ = 69-76)

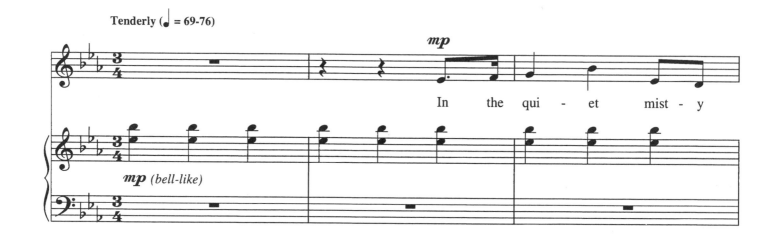

In the qui - et mist - y

morn - ing when the moon has gone to bed, when the spar - rows stop their

sing - ing and the sky is clear and red. When the

sum - mer's ceased its gleam - ing, when the corn is past its

prime, When ad - ven - ture's lost its mean - ing, I'll be

home - ward bound in time. Bind me not to the

pas - ture: chain me not to the plow. Set me

50

free to find my call - ing and I'll re - turn to you some - how.

If you find it's me you're miss - ing, if you're

hop - ing I'll re - turn. To your thoughts I'll soon be

list - 'ning in the road I'll stop and turn. Then the

* If breath is needed, take one here; otherwise, continue to end of phrase.

37 wind will set me rac - ing as my jour - ney nears its

cresc.

40 end, and the path I'll be re - trac - ing when I'm

mf *decresc.*

43 home - ward bound a - gain. Bind me not to the

mp *f* **45**

46 pas - ture; chain me not to the plow. Set me

free to find my call - ing and I'll re - turn to you some - how.

In the qui - et mist - y morn - ing when the moon has gone to

bed, when the spar - rows stop their sing - ing,

I'll be home - ward bound a - gain.

'CROSS THE WIDE MISSOURI

for solo voice with opitonal flute

Traditional
with additional words by
NANCY PRICE (ASCAP)

American folk songs
adapted and arranged by
DON BESIG (ASCAP)

* In absence of flute, play cues to m.7. Flute part on p. 62.

Copyright © MCMXCIII by Alfred Publishing Co., Inc.

11 'cross the wide Mis - sou -

14 In two (♩ = ca. 52) mf
ri. The wa - ter is

18 wide, I can - not get o'er.

Give me a boat _____ to take me ___ home. My true love waits _____ on yon - der __ shore, so far a - way, _____ so long a -

No more can I _____ be all a - lone. _____

_ My fu - ture waits _____ on yon - der ___

shore. Send me a boat _____

'CROSS THE WIDE MISSOURI

Traditional
with additional words by
NANCY PRICE (ASCAP)

American folk songs
adapted and arranged by
DON BESIG (ASCAP)

FLUTE

Jay Althouse

Jay Althouse received a D.O. degree in Music Education and a M.Ed degree in music from Indiana University of Pennsylvania. For eight years he served as a rights and licenses administrator for a major educational music publisher. During that time he served a term on the Executive Board of the Music Publishers Association of America.

As a composer of choral music, Jay has over 500 works in print for choirs of all levels. He is a writer member of ASCAP and is a regular recipient of the ASCAP Special Award for his compositions in the area of standard music.

His book, *Copyright: The Complete Guide for Music Educators, 2nd Edition*, is recognized as the definitive sourcebook on the subject of copyright for music educators. Jay has also co-written several songbooks, musicals, and cantatas with his wife, Sally K. Albrecht, and has compiled and arranged a number of highly regarded vocal solo collections. He is the co-writer of the best-selling book, *The Complete Choral Warm-Up Book*, published by Alfred. Most recently, he co-authored *Accent on Composers*, a reproducible sourcebook for classroom music teachers featuring the music and lives of 22 composers.

About the Recording

Folk Songs for Solo Singers, Vol. 1 accompaniment tracks were recorded at Red Rock Recording, Saylorsburg, PA

Piano - Sally K. Albrecht

Flute - Barb McMahon

Engineer - Kent Heckman

Many of the solos in this book are also available in choral editions from Alfred Publishing (see page 2). For a complete listing of Alfred Vocal Collections, please visit the Alfred website: www.alfred.com.